TOP 10 ANIMAL EXTREMES

THE 10 STRONGEST ANIMALS

BY RACHEL ROSE

BEARPORT PUBLISHING

Minneapolis, Minnesota

Credits
Cover and title page, © Design Pics Inc/Alamy Stock Photo, © DamianKuzdak/iStock, and © Hung Chung Chih/Shutterstock; Title Page, © Hung Chung Chih/Shutterstock; 4, © Yü Lan/Adobe Stock Photos; 5, © Mark Malkinson/Alamy Stock Photo; 6, © Frank Fichtmüller/iStock; 6–7, © Karine Patry/iStock; 8, © mirecca/Adobe Stock Photos; 9, © robertharding/Alamy Stock Photo; 10, © eco2drew/iStock; 11, © Franco Banfi/Blue Planet Archive; 12, © ANDREY GUDKOV/Alamy Stock Photo; 13, © robertharding/Alamy Stock Photo; 14, © NaturaLight/Alamy Stock Photo; 15, © All Canada Photos/Alamy Stock Photo; 16–17, © NSP-RF/Alamy Stock Photo; 17, © RainervonBrandis/iStock; 18, © Avalon.red/Alamy Stock Photo; 18–19, © Anup Shah/Getty Images; 20, © Nick Dale/Alamy Stock Photo; 20–21, © Design Pics Inc /Alamy Stock Photo; 22T, © chameleonseye/iStock; 22M, © Nature Picture Library/Alamy Stock Photo; 22B, © Ken Griffiths/iStock; 23, © EcoPic/iStock.

Bearport Publishing Company Product Development Team
Publisher: Jen Jenson; Director of Product Development: Spencer Brinker; Managing Editor: Allison Juda; Editor: Cole Nelson; Associate Editor: Naomi Reich; Associate Editor: Tiana Tran; Art Director: Colin O'Dea; Designer: Kim Jones; Designer: Kayla Eggert; Product Development Specialist: Owen Hamlin

Statement on Usage of Generative Artificial Intelligence
Bearport Publishing remains committed to publishing high-quality nonfiction books. Therefore, we restrict the use of generative AI to ensure accuracy of all text and visual components pertaining to a book's subject. See BearportPublishing.com for details.

Library of Congress Cataloging-in-Publication Data is available at www.loc.gov or upon request from the publisher.

ISBN: 979-8-89232-642-1 (hardcover)
ISBN: 979-8-89232-691-9 (ebook)

For more information, write to Bearport Publishing, 5357 Penn Avenue South, Minneapolis, MN 55419.

CONTENTS

MIGHTY BEASTS

There are millions of **species** of animals that make up the animal kingdom. They come in all shapes, colors, and sizes. Some are cute, some are gross, and some are deadly. But there are also a lot of animals that are super powerful.

WHAT ARE THE WILD WORLD'S 10 STRONGEST CREATURES?

Read on to decide for yourself. . . .

#10 HONEY BADGER

Don't be fooled by these cuties. Honey badgers may look adorable, but they are **fierce** and fearless. They will attack almost any animal—big or small. Honey badgers have a nasty bite and sharp claws to help them fight. The thick, loose skin around their necks protects them in a battle. In fact, their tough skin can even withstand **venomous** bites and stings.

#9 MUSK OX

Hands off! Male musk oxen, called bulls, will go to war for love. They butt heads topped in long, curved horns to battle it out to see which bull is strongest. These big beasts can ram into each other as many as 20 times! They continue running at each other at full speed—pushing heads and locking horns—until one of them backs down. Who's next?

Musk oxen also use their strong horns to protect their young.

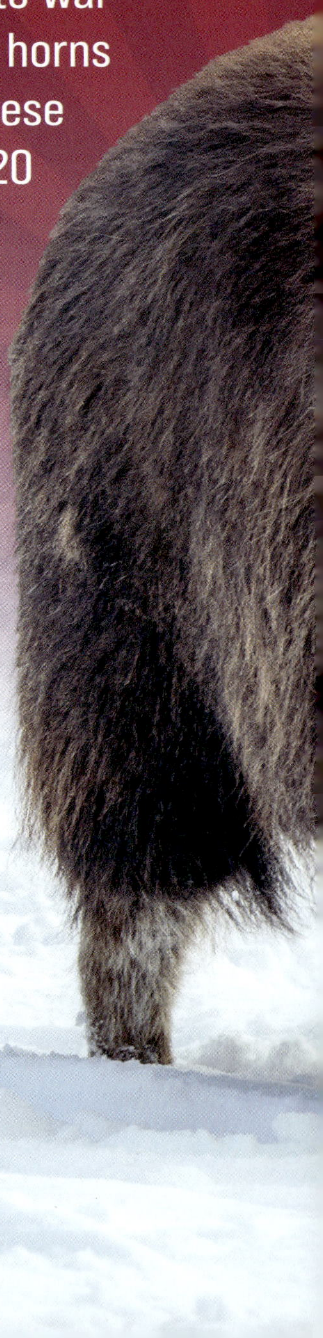

Bulls can weigh up to 800 pounds (360 kg).
Their predators include wolves and grizzly bears.
Sturdy legs help them move around their harsh Arctic homes.

#8 ELECTRIC EEL

Zap! The electric eel can deliver a shock that's strong enough to knock a horse off its feet. This shock tactic keeps predators at bay. Powerful **voltage** also helps the fish catch its **prey**. This zapper often wraps itself around a victim to increase the shock level. The electric eel's electricity is even stronger when leaping out of water!

#7 SPOTTED HYENA

Stay away! With their powerful jaws and teeth, spotted hyenas have one of the strongest bites of all **mammals**. This helps them feast on much larger animals, such as buffalos. First, these skilled hunters work together in small groups to find prey. Then, they attack—pouncing on their victims and gnawing through their bones. Dinner is served!

They sometimes munch on the leftovers from other animals.

Spotted hyenas can run for many miles at a time without getting tired.

They are also known as laughing hyenas because of the giggling sounds they make.

#6 BLUE WHALE

Blue whales are the largest animals that have ever lived, even bigger than dinosaurs! They can weigh as much as 200 tons (180 t). Blue whales have incredibly strong **muscles** that help them move their huge bodies through the water. A lot of their strength is in their tails. With just one powerful tail flick, these large creatures can finish off their predators!

These whales travel as far as 4,000 miles (6,400 km) when they **migrate**.

Thump-thump! A blue whale's heart weighs about the same as a small car.

Blue whales can hold a volume of water in their mouths greater than their own body weight.

Some blue whales have lived more than 100 years.

#5 GREEN ANACONDA

Watch out! While green anacondas are known for their supersize, they also have unbelievable strength. These powerful snakes can wrap their long bodies around prey much larger than themselves. Then, they squeeze with a force so hard that it feels the same as being crushed by a bus! *Ouch.*

Green anacondas hunt all kinds of animals, including wild pigs and caimans.

Sometimes, females eat males after they mate!

Green anacondas can weigh up to 550 lbs. (250 kg).

These snakes can open their jaws wide enough to swallow large prey whole.

#4 GRIZZLY BEAR

Bowling, anyone? Grizzly bears have a bite powerful enough to crush a bowling ball! They use their deadly jaws to hunt and catch salmon—their favorite food. But their strength doesn't end there. They also have extremely strong paws and sharp claws for digging deep dens. It can take them just days to dig out their cozy homes!

The bears' curved claws can be up to 4 in. (10 cm) long.

Grizzly bears are so strong that they have no natural predators.
This bear also uses the big hump on its back to dig its den.
A grizzly can lift up to 1,100 lbs. (500 kg).
Whether big or small, any animal can become a grizzly bear's dinner.

#3 DUNG BEETLE

Meet the world's strongest insect. One type of dung beetle can pull more than 1,000 times its own body weight. That's like a person pulling six double-decker buses at the same time! And what does the *dung* beetle pull? You guessed it . . . poop! This powerful insect rolls large balls of animal dung to store away for **future** meals.

Dung is another word for animal poop.

Sometimes, females lay their eggs in large poop balls.

They dig tunnels to store their balls of poo.

Relative to their size, dung beetles are among the strongest animals on Earth.

#2 MOUNTAIN GORILLA

Check out those muscles! Male mountain gorillas, or silverbacks, are the strongest of all apes. These mighty males are the leaders of their large family groups. They are responsible for protecting their families from predators and rival silverbacks. With their impressive arm strength, these apes can easily bend and snap trees. This helps them **forage** for food and get around in the dense forests where they live.

Silverback gorillas can weigh more than 400 lbs. (180 kg).

Thick fur helps them stay warm in cold temperatures.

A group of gorillas is called a troop.

Powerful arms and legs help these mighty animals climb trees.

#1 AFRICAN BUSH ELEPHANT

Stay back! Weighing in at about 14,000 lbs. (6,350 kg), the African bush elephant is the largest land animal on Earth. While a human has a mere 600 muscles in their entire body, an elephant's trunk alone contains 40,000 muscles! This big creature is so strong that it can pull a tree straight up out of the ground. Anybody need a mover?

African bush elephants uproot trees to eat the leaves and roots.

Strong jaws help the elephants chomp through tough plants—bark and all.

They live in African grasslands and deserts.

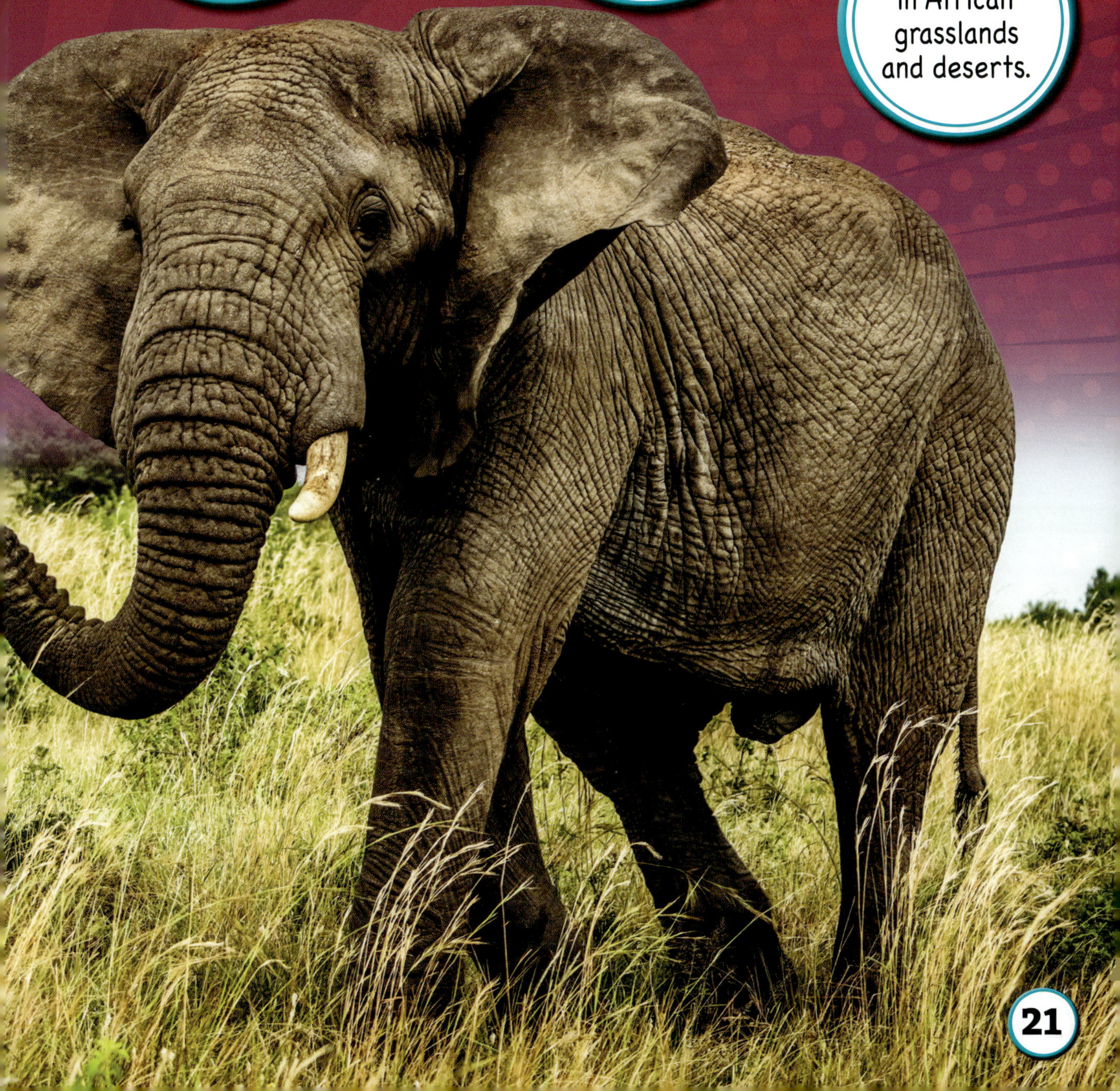

EVEN MORE STRONG ANIMALS

These 10 animals aren't the only mighty beasts in the wild. What others score high on the strength-o-meter?

SALTWATER CROCODILE

Be careful of snappy saltwater crocs in their watery **habitats**. These beasts have the strongest bite of any animal on Earth.

HARPY EAGLE

While soaring high in the sky, harpy eagles can carry up to twice their body weight. That makes them the strongest bird in the world.

LEAFCUTTER ANT

These critters can carry up to 50 times their body weight—in their mouths!

GLOSSARY

fierce dangerous and violent

forage to look for food in the wild

future a time that is going to happen later

habitats places in nature where animals or plants normally live

mammals warm-blooded animals that have hair, give birth to live young, and drink milk from their mothers as babies

migrate to move from one place to another at different times of the year

muscles parts of the body that make it move

predators animals that hunt and kill other animals for food

prey an animal that is hunted by another animal for food

species groups that animals are divided into, according to similar characteristics

venomous full of poison that is released through a sting or bite

voltage a unit for measuring electric strength

INDEX

READ MORE

Holmes, Kirsty. *Who's the Strongest? (Animal vs. Animal).* New York: Gareth Stevens Publishing, 2022.

Rose, Rachel. *Grizzly Bear (Library of Awesome Animals).* Minneapolis: Bearport Publishing Company, 2021.

LEARN MORE ONLINE

1. Go to **FactSurfer.com** or scan the QR code below.
2. Enter "**10 Strongest Animals**" into the search box.
3. Click on the cover of this book to see a list of websites.

ABOUT THE AUTHOR

Rachel Rose writes books for kids and teaches yoga. Her favorite animal for all time is her dog, Sandy.